ANGEL SHARPENING
ITS BEAK

BOOKS BY MICHAEL McGRIFF

Poetry
Dismantling the Hills
Home Burial
Early Hour
Eternal Sentences
Angel Sharpening Its Beak

Fiction
Our Secret Life in the Movies

As translator
The Sorrow Gondola by Tomas Tranströmer

As editor
To Build My Shadow a Fire: The Poetry and Translations of David Wevill

ANGEL SHARPENING
ITS BEAK

MICHAEL McGRIFF

Carnegie Mellon University Press
Pittsburgh 2025

ACKNOWLEDGMENTS

The author would like to thank the editors of the following journals where these poems first appeared:

Academy of American Poets, Poem-a-Day: "Men Keep on Dying"
The American Poetry Review: "Delivering Water to Glenbrook Nickel Co.," "To the Prairie, to the Ocean"
Harvard Review: "A Week Away from Quitting the Mill"
Orion: "Trying to Think" (under the title "After Watching Andrei Rublev, I Drive out into the Prairie, Trying to Think")
Quarterly West: "Playing Dead in the Field"
The Sewanee Review: "Wind"
Terrain: "An Offering"

The sequence "Black Postcards from Tenmile" and the poems "Our Water," "Property," and "Sitting Still" appear in the chapbook *Black Postcards* as Volume 7 of the Acme Poem Company Surrealist Poetry Series (Willow Springs Books, 2017).

"Animal Theory Along the Marys River," part 7 of the sequence "Corvus," appears in *Cascadia Field Guide: Art, Ecology, Poetry* (Mountaineers Books, 2023).

My deepest thanks to my writing group: Dorianne Laux, Joseph Millar, Sharon Olds, Major Jackson, Matthew Dickman, and Didi Jackson—theirs were the first eyes on many of these poems. Thanks, especially, to Joseph Millar, whose red pen and architectural vision ultimately gave this book its shape, tone, and narrative spine.

Thanks to Alexandra Teague and Cameron McGill for their exhaustive notes on the first completed version of this book.

Thanks to the University of Idaho for a 2023 sabbatical, which offered me the essential time and space to overhaul this collection.

Cover art: *Two Moons and Hole*, oil on linen, 40.5 x 30 cm, Chad Burt, 2014, courtesy of the artist and Herrmann Germann Conspirators, Zurich.

Book design by So Young Park

CONTENTS

PART ONE

OUR WATER

left the glasses cloudy
and stank of centipedes.
It bubbled from the ground
where the bears drank,
where the spring traps
held their mouths open
and the skunk cabbage
went crazy in the ravine.
My sister's hair turned the color
of a salamander's belly
and my teeth went gray
as the bathwater we all shared
on Sunday nights.
Our water, my father explained,
just ran a little rich.

PLAYING DEAD IN THE FIELD

Hay season. The men lean
against the split rail fence.
Even the oiled tongues of their boots
speak Finnish. The evening ridge
is a blue crown of deep hours.

For now, I belong to the quick mice,
and the wind is a smoky mirror
lowered onto the field.

A snake noses the low star
through the grass. In the sky,
five ticks filled with my blood
pulse between a man and his burden.

SHRAPNEL

When my grandfather flexed his jaw
the tip of a black horsehair
moved in his neck—mercurial,
visible, just beneath the skin.
The complete living motion
of an incomplete horse.
My birthmark, he said,
and made it sway
like blue ditch grass.
That dark star gave orders
to transport the dead
under the cover of slurry
the unlit sky had become.

CHARLENE

At the graveside funeral
you were in the nicest box
we could afford. Then

you were in a shore pine
banging a wooden spoon
against a stock pot.

How like you
to become the wind

and how like the wind
to scream backward
past the yields
and water tables
toward the first page
of the almanac.

GOING BACK

This is how it is—

We stumble to the river.
We have hay-lit faces.
The whole night runs with sap.

Our pant cuffs
fill with burs
and dead grass.

A red line is drawn tight
between low branches.

We hang our names
from gray clothespins.

The trees reach beyond
the turnbuckled dark
to drink the blood
of the moon.

A voice moves across the water
like a wedding dress
in a cedar chest,
like a season folded
into a black pocket square.

ASSEMBLING MY MOTHER

This bolt of sheer fabric.
I call it the body.

For the legs
I'll use sticks.

As for her lacquered
acrylic nails,
how could I ever
get those right?

She holds her hands
above her head
until a hardened star
replaces the tip
of each finger.

HIGH-WATER MARK

Five days of rain, and the dike road
losing ground to the river.

We work the low fields.
We chain stumps.
We pull and deeprut.
Light a slash pile with a flare gun.

River smoke and laughter.
We judder as God chips a tooth
against our ribs, as my father
turns a brake rotor for the last time.

PROPERTY

The deer cut a thin path
from the creek,
through the field,
along the crooked teeth of the fence,
past the stiff ears of the mule pen,
and into the underbrush
at the wood's edge.

The pipeline surveyors
have trespassed again, and again
I gather their bright flags.

The moon gathers evidence against us
and waits for its moment.

The path crawls from the creek
like a sentence
starting with the words
I wonder

and ending with a hooved ellipse
that bleeds into a clearing
circled by a stand of alders.

BURNED

for Alexandra Teague

What's written goes hollow, long-toothed, and mean.
The past is built by omission, its O
the same vowel that's soaked in gasoline.

We move beyond the facts, beyond the seen.
We migrate at night, like birds—no, like blood.
What has teeth gets written, hollow and mean.

I adore the singed list of a crow's wing.
I deny the charred matchstick of the known.
I'm nothing but the smell of gasoline.

Our home town?—the everything of nothing
where my mouth's black wing is pinned down and sewn
to what's written, hollow, long-toothed, and mean.

We lurk and siphon and laugh at the sting
while others deny and deny what we know:
we'll never lose the taste for gasoline.

We are lean, we are boys with blind swinging
fists, we are sand and gravel, we are home.
What's written goes hollow, long-toothed, and mean.
Nothing beats the pull of sweet gasoline.

AN OFFERING

If I were the type to look for a sign,
I might turn to the wet Coleman sleeping bag
in the bed of my truck, which is now
a motor lodge for worms and centipedes,
or I might consider the '74 de Ville limousine
parked forever in our neighbor's yard,
an orange life jacket hung from its boomerang antenna
like a horseshoe thrown by a drunken god.
But I'm not the type. I am moved, however,
to say something about the alders,
which are incandescent bones—
for ten years, while my father got ready for work,
it was my job to shovel the cold ash
from our woodstove and dump it at their feet.

SIXTEEN WITH BLOWN HEAD GASKET, NORTH OF MADRAS

The red wind with all
its desert catchphrases.
It has no horizon.
It rocks my '78 Datsun.
What passes for rain
bubbles up on the dust.

I stare down the scrub trees
which move like teeth worked loose
with a dry tongue.

If you said I could cheat death
by naming the animal
these roadside tracks belong to,
I'd take a stab—wild turkey, coyote,
one-legged ghost—and I'd be wrong.
How many seconds years dreams ago
did they move deeper
into this canyon's draw?

My radiator's hissing
and the hood's propped up
in its best imitation of a cormorant's wing
in a landscape no cormorant
would fly near enough to curse.

I know to drive with the heater on,
that I must first sit and wait
for the hours to grow cool
to the touch.

But here's what I don't yet know:
this is all there is, this altar of my life.

PART TWO

BLACK POSTCARDS FROM TENMILE

for Gray Jones

1. Hag's Inlet

The waters bent
to their purpose

and the silt thickblack
as a dog's tongue.

The rain, a jar of rivets
emptied onto a sheet of tin.

I've lost so many things
beneath the moon's old rags
rotting in these shore pines,

yet I can always find
the same good screwdriver
for shucking oysters,

can always see
the three colors of death
gleam in a horse's eye:
honing oil, carbide, and strop.

2. Echoes

The past is free
but the future
will cost you,

the moon says,
reflecting the bonfire
back to us.

A hoof enters the creek,
the coals are raked,
the barnlight shatters
into corn silk
across the night waters
then regathers its contradictions.

3. Blood Harmony

How could I not admire
the brothers up the road
throwing fistfuls of gravel
at the cars, which pass by
so infrequently that I feel
like an outboard motor
clamped to a sawhorse.

4. Night Geese over the North Spit

Like the night, bone unto bone,
my left side is held together
with seven pins and sixteen screws.

The sky turns through its hours
and I moan like the iron bands
around an oak barrel
filled with cigarettes, oyster shells,
and rainwater.

Some things you don't unhear—
night geese, wind through a floorboard
on the day of a funeral.
Aksel, without ceremony,
dropping his father's glass eye
down the Corsons' well.

5. Shore Wind

Each year, what remains of my life
becomes shredded in the wind
like a tarp weighted down over a roof
with milk jugs filled with sand.

And if there's a name
for what turns the new planks gray
and makes the old planks complain
through the seasons,
I don't want—not now, not ever—
to know enough to know it.

6. *Still Life*

The moon ground down
to its aggregate
and polished hitch-bright
on the sleeve of a drunk
who's just lain down
in his neighbor's horse trailer.

7. *To Approximate a Swainson's Thrush*

Toss a Chevy's coil spring from the trestle
then turn its echo into black waves

then back into the black of everything
more likely heard than seen.

8. *Prosody*

There's nothing left for me here
but death's zip code
and the moon scoured and arranged
until it's clean and irrelevant
as the bone and coral inlays
of a belt buckle tossed
into a box.

9. Audit of Sky & Trestle

The night on the wind
like a voice through a bedroom wall
stuffed with newspaper and straw.

As the train approached,
your shadow stretched
all the way up the dunes.

You became a man on stilts
in the backcountry of the afterlife,
a blue star hidden in each fist,
the wind tearing up the grass
by the roots, and the sky
grown suddenly smaller.

10. Night Sky over Tenmile Creek

Finally, we're drunk enough
to keep the bonfire
chasing the stars back
to their side of the fence.

11. Near Milepost 223

Translate the coyote
through all the languages

of the night
and you're left
with a crow's black legs
or the pastern of a horse.

This explains
the coyote's long volleys
from the moonshadow
scalloped across the dunes,
which happily explains
nothing at all.

PART THREE

AFTER AN UNINSURED VISIT WITH A SURGEON,
I STOP BY CENTRAL DOCK

I stare at this deepwater vessel
docked and so immense
that I can't name a thing.
Painted on its hull,
something in Mandarin,
and I'd like to think it says
For you, who are looking now . . .
Of course, it is, essentially, nothing,
just as I am nothing
to the man who's scheduled a day
and time to cut into me
and then complain at lunch
that I'm just another insurance write-off
with a name unremarkable
as a mailbox or milepost.
I carry a small admiration
for how fresh lumber turns gray
after a single, uneventful season
of slack water, missed appointments,
and rubber boots slumped
near the back door.
Dear sound of mooring rope,
tell me: what ever happened
to Hunchback Charlie,
who I framed houses with,
who never missed a chance to complain
that Capitalism was a terminal illness
and then ate lunch alone in his Tercel
praying to catch it? And why

does this brackish water lapping
an iron hull remind me of such men?
I have a small flutter in my eye.
I am not tired. I'm not even
particularly lonely or bored
or moved by the desire
to be elsewhere.
There's a machine in me
no bigger than a cat's skull—
I hear how it fills with blood,
assembling its case notes
for a jury of my peers. This wind,
so slight, just barely enough
to make the dark water shine
if you know how to hold still
and look beyond all names
and into the constant light
anchored against the tide.

MEMORY & TROUGH

We were strictly forbidden
to drink from the trough,
but I won my bets
by plunging headfirst
up to my shoulders.
What they never understood—
I could stay down there for days.
I knew I'd reenter the world
as a story that would crawl
like ice from a burst pipe,
sheering off the fittings
and eating all the threads
while the human world slept.

DELIVERING WATER TO GLENBROOK NICKEL CO.

for Joseph Millar

I carry five-gallon jugs up the stairs
of the nickel plant. *Red clouds*
with a chance of dust—the same joke
every week from a wild man, goggles
loose at his neck. This is 1996.
I idle in my stepside, separate the pink
and yellow invoices. Beside me,
a Russian novel, the first book
I've ever tried to read. When I touch it,
an old woman praises the blank tongues
of a cabbage, far from here . . .
All over town, the light keeps
putting words in the landscape's mouth.
What was a season is now just a flicker
on a navigational buoy, and I become
the sound of a chipped teakettle
as the old woman reaches for the handle
in the dark. Maybe one day I'll understand
why she's never given a name.
I start the truck. I'm waved through the gate.
Red dust, red dust, as if termites gnawed the mudsill
from every word I'll bring to this memory.

ANGEL SHARPENING ITS BEAK

I'm a bright animal in a broken field.
But in memory, I'll become the broken animal
in a bright field. Why the constant desire
for revision? Lately, my contempt riots after sundown.
I reach up and unscrew the stars from their sockets.
The fir tree polishes a lost bell
as a final gesture of evening—I name it and mock it, here.
For what?—its excess? its desire and flare?
I know so little about the history of the terra-cotta
soldier and his horse. But I once saw
a fenceless horse throwing sparks from its hooves,
at night, on a gravel road, crossing so many property lines.
To write it, diminishes it. That's certain.
It's no secret I keep a sewing kit
of feathers under my wing. The same truck
passes by my window, as it has at all hours,
for months now. It's nothing sinister,
just my scrappy neighbor of the 10,000 jobs.
The sound of an angel sharpening its beak
is again just coffee percolating on the stove.
I reach for it. I reach for it without language.

SITTING STILL

I drive to town
in an hour bled free
of its light.

The traffic signals
blink yellow
and the fog turns
on its lathe.

I park in the back lot
of Warehouse Foods
and smoke in my truck,
the nickel plant
across the slough
in its jagged garland
of floodlights.

The night waters
are gray flux scrambling
the moon's bad hip.

Earlier, before we started
drinking, my mother and I
sat in the kitchen
and she sorted
through a shoebox
full of pill bottles.
I wanted her to sit still
so I could paint
her shadow onto the wall.

MEN KEEP ON DYING
for Denis Johnson

The stranger bites into an orange
and places the rind between us
on the park bench.
It becomes a small raft of fire.

I came here to admire
the iron-lit indifference
of the geese on the pond.

The summers here
are a circuit in parallel
with everything I cannot say
wrote the inventor
before he was hanged
from the bridge
this park is named after.
His entire life devoted
to capturing inextinguishable light
in a teardrop of enamel.
He was hanged for touching
the forehead of another man
in the wrong century.

The only thing invented
by the man I lost yesterday
was his last step into a final
set of parenthesis.
I came here to watch the geese
and think of him.
The stranger and I

share the orange rind
as an ashtray.
He lights my cigarette
and the shadows of our hands
touch on the ground.

His left leg is amputated
below the knee
and the bell tower rings
above the town.
I tell him my name
and he says nothing.

With the charred end of a stick
something shaped like a child
on the other side of the pond
draws a door on a concrete wall
and I wonder where the dead
wait in line to be born.

OF BARNS & BARNWOOD

Now, a chain and tow hook
are all it takes to pull one
to its knees. They're sold at auction
for the quaint gray wood
where nobody knows the mink oil
of my grandmother's tongue.

I'll spend December staring
into the trough where no animals
have gathered for a generation—
when a blue star falls into it
I'll see the rags of my face
bloom in the water. It is over,
it is all over when everything
becomes the motion of snow
gathering in the ditch of a memory
just out of reach.

A WEEK AWAY FROM QUITTING THE MILL

Container ship, deadpan clouds.
In ten minutes, we'll punch in
for the day shift.

I thread new orange laces
through the eyelets of my boots,
as if the old machines
won't make cripples of us all.

Just outside the break room,
a few birds work through
a drought equation,
an order of operations
involving dust and dead grass,
low water and paid time off.

Even though the wind draining the color
from a fence post is another way
to calculate the rate at which
I remain in this life, I have something
best thought of as wonder
as I take my place on the line.

THE GRAMMAR OF THE MORNING

The season's down on its haunches.
The light in the stockyard, all splay and echo.
I read a book where ice glistens like lard.
I walk to work and pass the hospital's
medical waste dumpster,
two grain elevators, and the beauty school.
Sometimes I cross the empty lot
where the city dumps its black snow.
The lines across my face
are a wiring schematic
for an irrelevant machine.
Aging, a cruel efficiency
I've come to accept and admire.
Before this gets too serious,
you should know that I'll never
be the kind of person
who feeds a wounded animal
with an eye dropper.
Nor will I lend the stars
any fatalistic agency
or study a fistful of bones
thrown to the floor.
On the radio, our lieutenant governor
answers a question with a question.
Evasion as a kind of shimmy
in a time of violence, the comma
before the conjunction.

POEM OF SIMILITUDE

This morning light, so singular in its purpose,
like a leather strop or a butcher's scale.

Amniotic light, the light of slow horses,
a light that says *Come on, double down, the fix is in.*

Today, I'm going off script. I'm gathering up
this unraveled dress masquerading as the morning
and drawing it near.

Last night, after we read a book
where a talking weasel again
made his improbable escape, my son asked
When you're dead, will I have a father?

I didn't say *No.* Nor did I say
All you'll have is the ache of similitude.
Nor *Like all sons, you'll pick your teeth
with the slender bone of the world.*

DRIVING HOME

Today, a tarp snagged on a wire fence
along I-84, shredded into what could be
a mystic's forbidden robe whose color
also describes my grandfather's eyes,
which constantly leaked like the stalks
of some ditch weed broken open.

My son, dreaming and contorted
in the back seat, my wife lost
in an endless book from the '20s,
my mind a steaming bale of hay
in a landscape I can't leave.

The river, just out of sight.
The moon, on the edge of rising,
looking to turn us all
into its unwitting collaborators.
The backs of my hands look, now,
like my father's—short-fingered,
arthritic, crazy-veined, and blue

as this blue tarp no one
will care enough to remove
from the hands of the wind
or the mind that turns it into a word
like *umbrage*, which means one thing
and its near opposite.

PART FOUR

CORVUS

1. Morning Query

If you ever see the sun calcify along the ridge,
if you ever see a boy squatting in a parking lot
behind a dusty evergreen shrub, scratching his name
into a window with a piece of gravel,
and if that window belongs to the King's Table
all-you-can-eat buffet on Bayshore and 7th,
don't dishonor me by alerting the shift manager,
and don't denigrate the past—or desire—
by mocking the two-for-one special.

I woke up at 4:00 this morning to a crow
imitating a woodpecker and asked myself
the question the crow seemed to propose
to the chilled, carbonized air:
Am I inert or expanding?

So, I ask the boy, and he carries on with his work,
suspicious as always, hunched there
as he's been for the past forty-five years,
of those who deny or neglect their helplessness.

2. Hatch & Crow

After the final thaw of the season,
a green midge-flare from the ditch.
Thunderheads stack above the crow

whose reflection crosses
the oiled skin of my coffee
while it cools in my hands.

3. Movement in an Unremarkable Hour

Our dead neighbor is wheeled
on a gurney from her house.
I mistake this for movers
and a service van. We thought
we knew her. We thought
we knew something about crows.
But they don't collect coins or old keys
or scraps of tinfoil from the trash.
They gather what is necessary,
nothing more. They gather near.
When our son hears them bicker
he says *Can you hear that scarecrow
crying?* They are in the trees.
They are on the roof.
They drop their black flags,
despite us. And despite us,
he is waiting for an answer.

4. Self-Portrait with Black Cup

This hubcap? It's called a *baby moon, a moonie,
a smoothie,* and even here, in it,

I watch my face outsourcing its own beauty.
I'm sure someone has an equation
suggesting I'm not looking into a hubcap
but, rather, into a dog's polished tooth
in another dimension.
What good is such an idea, really,
right now, in such a country?
It's a new season, and my thoughts
are not my thoughts, is all I can think.
In the next three months the light here
will be too low to reach my window.
It knows that I'm the type of person
who orders the cheapest item on the menu,
that I'm principled in anonymity.
The dead crow and its jackknifed voice
are on display on my front steps.
I can hear it. It's raising a toast. It's waiting
for me with a cultured irreverence
as I open all the cupboards
in every house I've ever lived
to find just the right black cup.

5. *Imposter*

I pretend I'm visiting the earth
in the shape of a paper crown
but everyone knows
I'm the dirt eater
of a dirt eater

of a dirt eater
who confuses *epithet*
with *epaulet*.
When I prance around
the scrapyard I'd rather press
two gas caps together and *caw*
than stare into the smelter
of a crow's hinged face.
Who am I
to be this far removed
from the vernacular
of its foot?

6. Memorial Day

We, the dead, the wind declares
without finishing its sentence.

Everyone I pass in the neighborhood
this morning feels like some kind of underpass
the wind screws its mouth to
so it can practice a single note.

If you ask what I'm thinking
as the wind blows rain against the house
I'll say a white lottery ball stowed away
in a crow's beak. Also, how that reminds me
of the smell of sulfur on a matchstick
when dragged across a zipper,

how the trilliums get dressed
for the work they carry out, without
complaint, in a ditch filling with water,
slowly, slowly, as the living grow fewer.

7. Crow's Feet

I watch eight crows
peck and tear into the death-bloat
of a sea lion, its tail torn free,
the fore flippers gone,
the hind flippers and head,
long gone. More sculpture
than animal, all self-tomb,
king tide, and shine.

You crows, feasting,
not like fools nor gentry,
but the measure of all things.
To think I've had the gall
to liken the skin about my eyes
to your feet. How is it I ever
drew them into comparison?—
those death hooks anchored
to stench and blubber,
those grapnels and flesh flukes,
the ruckus of purpose.

8. Animal Theory Along the Marys River

I write *The sun calcifies along the ridge* . . .

but maybe I mean *I've awakened
into the prime of my own mediocrity* . . .

Sound travels far here.
A cultivator tine hits red clay
a few acres downriver

or maybe it's the carrion snap
of a crow pulling a coyote's tendon
over a kind of hollow instrument
the low moon has made of us all . . .

Farm kids whisper over a little tent of sticks,
a book of matches, a clump of hair . . .

A question I refused to listen to, once,
in a moment of consequence, finally reaches me—
that, too, is a sound I've learned to ignore,
like a wall clock or the coarse paper
the dead fold into ridiculous swans . . .

Who am I to write *The sun calcifies along the ridge* . . . ?
King Fucking Nobody, that's who. But it's not so bad
to enter into one's irrelevancy, to become a kind
of mannered longhand, an abacus, the return spring
in a rotary dial . . .

What's certain is that we live
in an age of certainty.

What's certain is that my qualifications
for this life include
replacing the real with anything
but the real.

The apogee of a star searching for still water.
A pillow filled with blue down and regret.

A list in search of items is all I am
when sitting near long grasses and sourcane
along the riverbank.

I tilt my crown of roots
and become a thrush, a dirigible, an apple . . .
or an animal that eats gravel
to break down the food in its gut.

Why know the names of things
when you can imagine that *corvus*
means *memory eater* in Latin?

Dear Landscape . . .
Dear Life in Bold Letters, why has my friend
been forced to kill, breaking down doors
at given sets of coordinates
in a country whose name has made a career
of being mispronounced on public television?

Forgive me, whoever you are, I know it's inconvenient
to think about the poor and their tasks.

My task is to brood and wander,
and why should you care?

I'm talking with friends
and the air's finally cool
and the river's music has dampened,
still and flat . . .

I started with *The sun calcifies along the ridge*

but really I meant *I love the world most*
when animals serve as mere ornamentation.

They froth at the ends of their chains and bang
their bone plates against the unmarked crates
in my heart.

The wind is green.
Larval husks rattle in the wheeling air.

I am home.
I have everything
I've ever wanted
or mourned.
I take my assigned seat
in the order of the evening.

A crow plays a bit role
with its small complaint—

and what I admire most
is that it remains a thing
I've never fully seen,
even though, without thinking,
I polish it to an unnatural shine
with all the rags and ash
that fall from the moon-bleached
and darkening trees

as a few feet from us all, a single mooring cleat
holds the universe in its place.

PART FIVE

RAIN

Old floor plank,
I know it's too late,
but I'm home again
trying not to waken you.

Still, don't forget
the way
I stepped around
your dark note
all those years

looking for rats
to drown
in a bucket
of dead water.

TO THE PRAIRIE, TO THE OCEAN

for Robert Wrigley

At Inland Farm & Feed
I mistake *salt* for *suet* on my list
and remember how we
called my uncle *Turkey Pecker*
and the *Surgeon of Sturgeon*.
When he disappeared
I was told he was a deckhand
lost in the Bering Sea.
Really, he was serving time
for a string of petty offenses.
Or was it arson and larceny?
How easily one name,
one kindness, one offense
replaces another, a kind
of common erasure
named like a lipstick:
Shadow upon Shadow.
All this rolling prairie dropping
into the tinderbox canyons
of central Idaho
and it's the first summer
in forty-three years
I won't see the ocean.
Is it suet or salt,
pelagic or prairie?
Or is my longing, like a name,
both the arc of a wave
and the surge of its shadow?
Ocean, it's here that I address you:

What are your gray shoulders
charging into right now?
What shore animal watches you
dismantle yourself
against the jetty
then dance
into self-assembly?
Shadow upon shadow.
To burn through each integer
of every coordinate.
To be a descendent of nothing
and mouthpiece
for no one. Tell me,
where do I sign?
How singular you are
in your purpose,
how detached from the desire
to tell or to name,
and how averse to description,
finally, you actually are.
If I wrote a letter
that would carry me back to you,
I might start by writing,
Dear Gearbox of the Dead . . .
Dear Alkaline Ghost . . .
Dear Star-Eater No Aperture Can Hold . . .
Loneliness, like salt, like water,
needs no similitude.
Soon, I'll drive toward the desert

where the fast-growing trees
are harvested from merciless
irrigated rows to become
pulped and pressed
into the furniture of the poor,
so much cheap shelving
that a single cup of water
and something as elegant
and careless as the human hand
can so casually destroy.

BURN PILE

In this mineral season
the flowers are dethroned
and so many distances compete
for the slate light
before the snows begin.

I'm burning dry rot, beetle-kill,
a bag of junk mail.

Earlier, I watched earth haulers
crawl down the rings of a pit mine
as one thumbprint of rain
disappeared into the mountains.

What is the name of my crime
that I seek out such gradation of color
and bitter composition?

I locate three stars to the north.
They are riderless.
Smudged glass. The motion
from a dream escaped of its sleeper.
I call this constellation
The Copper Horse
or My Last Drink.

But I know it, too,
is merely smoke
backstitched
across the gathering night.

TRYING TO THINK

The sky is a featherless color
no floral dress can pass through
or impress, and this darkening hour
tilts on its fulcrum, beyond thought,
at the edge of town,
where a kestrel waits in a cow's shadow
among the stubble-ruin.

There's much to admire
in these gray outbuildings,
which resemble in their airy lilts
and crippled shoulders
the old women of my childhood
who poured warm oils into my ears
after I swam the fever waters
of the mill pond.

At sixteen, I parked at the Salt Gulch Substation
with the windows down and the lights cut
so I could taste the current in the air
and feel the logging ridges rise up
in every direction.

But now, I'm driving away from a gas station
with three lottery tickets and a bag of peanuts,
and the light across the county
is flat as a milk-dead eye. The prairie grass
holds the patterns of a dry wind in search of fire
and my body fills with an iron bell,
poorly cast, a wild bit of rope
pulling at a darkness.

FEBRUARY TRUCK STOP

Wind in a low place.
A distance between Tallow Ridge
and Nerval Draw
measured in bruised light.

Trees howl through
the weather, ditch-dark clouds
touch the ground, and two men,
from one diesel pump
to another, shout something
about the *erotic pines*

and *the sum of heaven.*
Their voices wrung out,
punched through, full of snow
and glitter-slick miles.
I consider nothing
of the days before
or the days to come.

Trucks chain up across the road.
Rigs crawling down from the summit
smell of hot brakes and spoiled fish.

The erotic pines.
The sum of heaven.
Voices cross a cement slab
and find each other.
I raise a hand to each,
as is the way here,
then get back in my truck.

THINKING OF HOME IN THE HOUR
OF TRANSFORMATIONS

Walking beneath a greased moon
on a street named for Indian killers
in a town I've tried and failed to love,
I'm suddenly thirty years younger
lying awake in a hush
which is also the sound of Catching Slough,
a landscape adrift
in the absence of language
where I stand behind long curtains
trying to capture a paper wasp
between an empty glass
and a postcard I've received
from a dead relative, a wailing
and the sound of water
deep at the back of it all.

WIND

When the dead unbury themselves,
will they finally throw away
all the chipped saucers
and scrape the contact paper
from the cupboards,
will they awaken
into the ceremonies
their bad knees and small regrets
have become? Like me,
will they keep their heads down
at the grocery store, avoiding
conversations with others?

I remember, now,
when rat piss, hay, and stars
all smelled the same

and how the barn sang
in the wind,
and how no one cared
if I slept there all night
without naming any of it
or wanting it named
or wanting anything at all.

READING THE CLASSIFIEDS ON MILL ROAD

This light
across the silt beds—
unceremonial, jimmied
into place, out of style
yet oracular.
To describe it
runs a grease rag over it.
If nothing else,
this light holds the scrapyard together.
It makes the chains call
to the load binder.
It tricks the gravel
into undressing
before the dusty mirror
of my thought.
With the *Nickel Shopper*
spread across the steering wheel
and the window cracked,
I hear a voice rise up
from a cigarette burn
in the seat. So *this*
is the voice of God?
No, just the silence here
pinned to a windless day
of little consequence
where the mind asserts
its patterns and voices.
Old appliances.
A horse trailer
you can have for free

if you haul it off.
I fold the paper back
into its square
and think of boats
and crowns
the dead might make.
It's true, I think of them,
here, in this place,
with their bad teeth
and accents
who've become
the fists of stubbled wheat
beneath the snow.
I unwind my roll
of Lion Mints,
tamp a pack of smokes
against the dash.
Three times for luck
and once for the dead.
I turn the key.
I pull on the lights.
I pass into the absolute
color beneath the hour.